GREEN POWER

Nick Winnick

j333.799
WIN

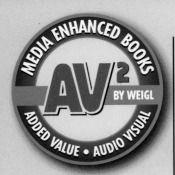

AV² by Weigl brings you media enhanced books that support active learning.

AV² provides enriched content that supplements and complements this book. Weigl's AV² books strive to create inspired learning and engage young minds for a total learning experience.

Go to **www.av2books.com**, and enter this book's unique code. You will have access to video, audio, web links, quizzes, a slide show, and activities.

BOOK CODE

M760970

Audio
Listen to sections of the book read aloud.

Video

Web Link
Find research sites and play interactive games.

Try This!
Complete activities and hands-on experiments.

Due to the dynamic nature of the Internet, some of the URLs and activities provided as part of AV² by Weigl may have changed or ceased to exist. AV² by Weigl accepts no responsibility for any such changes. All media enhanced books are regularly monitored to update addresses and sites in a timely manner. Contact AV² by Weigl at 1-866-649-3445 or av2books@weigl.com with any questions, comments, or feedback.

Published by AV² by Weigl
350 5th Avenue, 59th Floor
New York, NY 10118
Website: www.av2books.com   www.weigl.com

Library of Congress Cataloging-in-Publication Data available upon request.
Fax 1-866-44-WEIGL for the attention of the Publishing Records department.

ISBN 978-1-61690-097-7 (hard cover)
ISBN 978-1-61690-098-4 (soft cover)

Printed in the United States of America in North Mankato Minnesota
1 2 3 4 5 6 7 8 9 0   14 13 12 11 10

062010
WEP264000

Project Coordinators: Heather C. Hudak, Robert Famighetti
Design: Terry Paulhus
Project Editor: Emily Dolbear
Photo Research: Edward A. Thomas
Layout and Production: Tammy West

CONTENTS

MAKING THE WORLD A GREENER PLACE

How can you make the world a greener place? You can help the planet by reducing your **carbon footprint**. A carbon footprint is the measure of **greenhouse gases** produced by human activities.

Greenhouse gases are produced by burning **fossil fuels**. People burn fossil fuels for electricity, heating, and powering vehicles. One of the biggest causes of climate change is the greenhouse gas known as **carbon dioxide**. Many scientists believe that carbon **emissions** are more damaging to Earth than any other kind of pollution.

There are many ways you can reduce your carbon footprint. One way is to walk or ride your bike instead of riding in a car. You can turn off lights when you leave a room to reduce energy waste. Reusing plastic shopping bags to carry other items is another way to help the environment. You can **recycle** newspaper so that fewer trees are chopped down to make new paper.

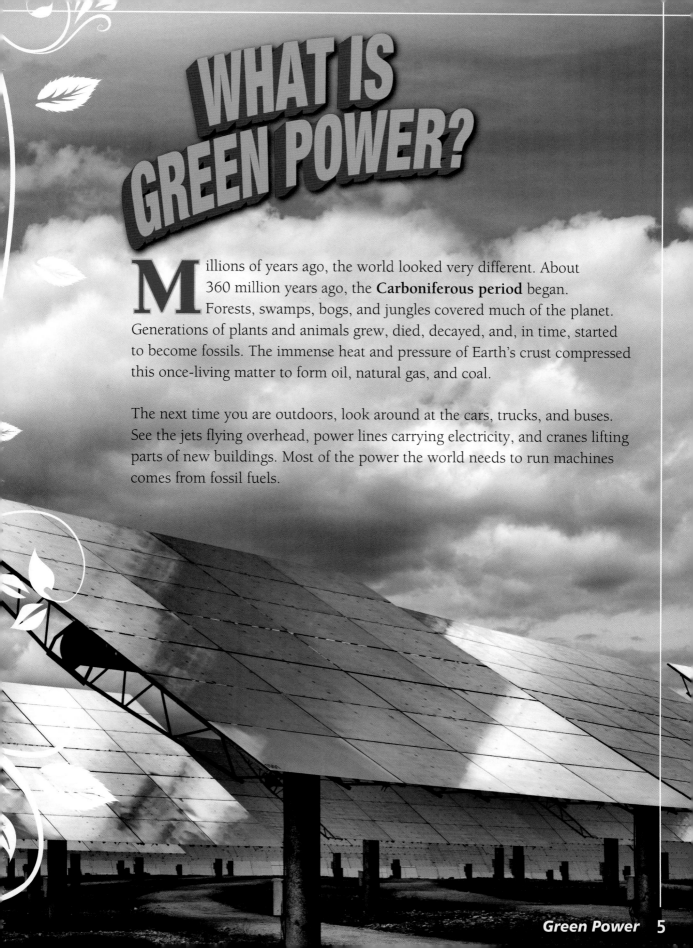

WHAT IS GREEN POWER?

Millions of years ago, the world looked very different. About 360 million years ago, the **Carboniferous period** began. Forests, swamps, bogs, and jungles covered much of the planet. Generations of plants and animals grew, died, decayed, and, in time, started to become fossils. The immense heat and pressure of Earth's crust compressed this once-living matter to form oil, natural gas, and coal.

The next time you are outdoors, look around at the cars, trucks, and buses. See the jets flying overhead, power lines carrying electricity, and cranes lifting parts of new buildings. Most of the power the world needs to run machines comes from fossil fuels.

1 POWERING THE FUTURE

Humans have depended on fossil fuels for more than a century. They will soon need to find cleaner, more **sustainable** sources of power to maintain their way of life.

REASONS TO USE GREEN ENERGY

Reduce the Need for Fossil Fuels

People are using fossil fuels faster than Earth can generate them. Some experts believe it will take decades to run out of oil and more than 50 years to deplete natural gas reserves. Supplies of coal may last for more than a century. Still, at some point, these fuel supplies will run out. What kind of energy do you think might one day replace fossil fuels?

> "The human race is challenged more than ever before to demonstrate our mastery—not over nature but of ourselves."
>
> –Rachel Carson, American biologist and author

Lower Rising Fuel Costs

Filling up a car with gasoline, heating a home with natural gas, and using coal-generated electricity is more expensive than ever. It is hard to imagine how those costs could decrease. When fossil fuel prices rise, other prices, such as those for food, construction, and transportation, rise as well. What price increases have you noticed?

Decrease Carbon Dioxide Levels

Fossil fuels contain carbon. During the Carboniferous period, plants took carbon dioxide gas from the **atmosphere** and stored the carbon in their tissues. Humans have already released at least half of that stored carbon back into the atmosphere. The release of carbon dioxide into the atmosphere contributes to an increase in Earth's average temperature.

2 PHOTOVOLTAIC SOLAR

T he Sun is shining somewhere on Earth every minute of every day, providing energy. One of the most popular green technologies are solar cells, or photovoltaic cells. They use the Sun's energy to directly produce electricity.

WAYS TO USE PHOTOVOLTAIC SOLAR POWER

Create Photovoltaic Power Plants

Photovoltaic cells, or PV cells, convert sunlight directly into electricity. Scientists used **silicon** to create the first useful, electric-generating photovoltaic cell in 1954. People use PV cells in many different ways, including large-scale power plants and wristwatches. Have you ever used a calculator that did not need batteries? It used PV cells to run. What other items do you use that have PV cells?

> "Do not go where the path may lead; go instead where there is no path and leave a trail."
> –Ralph Waldo Emerson, American poet

Build with PV Cells

Green construction uses solar technology as part of a building's walls, rooftops, and windows. PV cells become part of the building's construction. The U.S. Department of Energy has estimated that building-integrated photovoltaics (BIPV) technology could one day generate half of the electrical needs in the United States. What kind of buildings in your community might have been built with PV cells?

Use Thin-Film Solar Panels

A new development in photovoltaic solar energy is thin-film solar cells. Thin-film solar panels produce less electricity per square foot (meter) than other solar panels. However, they are also much cheaper to make. Unlike solar panels, which are bulky and stiff, thin-film panels roll off the assembly line like paper off a printing press. Thin-film solar cells are so light and flexible that they cover U.S. Army tents to provide soldiers with a local power source. What other ways could people use thin-film solar panels?

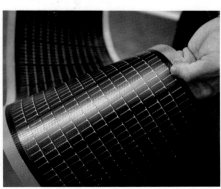

3 SOLAR THERMAL

Turning the Sun's energy directly into electricity is not the only way to take advantage of the power of the Sun. Energy from sunlight can also be trapped as heat. Solar thermal power uses heat to run a special type of machine that produces electricity.

WAYS TO USE SOLAR THERMAL ENERGY

Develop More Solar Thermal Power Plants

One type of solar thermal collector is a curved reflector, such as a mirror or polished metal. The reflector focuses light from the Sun on a container filled with fluid. The focused sunlight

heats the fluid inside the container. The heat from this fluid produces steam that turns machines called turbines. This generates electricity. Kramer Junction in California's Mojave Desert is home to one of the world's largest solar thermal power plants.

"More energy from the Sun hits Earth in one hour than all of the energy consumed by humans in an entire year....The majority of life on Earth is already solar powered—why aren't we?"

–Kerry Dunnington, caterer and author

Use Solar Thermal Heat at Home

Some solar thermal systems at home collect and use the Sun's heat directly. Solar collectors are used to heat water, which is then used for cooking, cleaning, and bathing. The water can also be sent through pipes and radiators to heat the buildings themselves. How might heating a home with solar power be a challenge?

Cook with the Sun

Some solar collectors serve as ovens or stoves to cook food. The ancient Greeks recognized they could use the power of the Sun to light fires and to cook. What ways could you use solar thermal energy?

4 USING HYDROPOWER

The movement of water in rivers or over waterfalls contains huge amounts of energy. Constructing barriers, or dams, in the paths of waterways allows humans to harvest this energy to produce electricity. One of the world's major barriers is Hoover Dam, which was built across the Colorado River in 1936.

REASONS TO BUILD HYDROELECTRIC DAMS

Provide Renewable Energy Electrical power generated from the force of falling or flowing water is called **hydroelectricity**. In 2008, hydroelectricity accounted for the largest share of all **renewable**-generated electricity in the United States. In fact, it is the world's largest renewable energy source. Today, the largest U.S. hydroelectric dam is the Grand Coulee Dam in Washington. Find out if your state has any hydroelectric plants you could visit.

"This morning I came, I saw, and I was conquered, as everyone would be who sees for the first time this great feat of mankind."
–*President Franklin Delano Roosevelt, at the Hoover Dam dedication*

Keep It Clean Hydropower produces no greenhouse gases. However, creating dams requires moving rivers and streams artificially, which can damage local **ecosystems**. All new dams must be designed and built with care and attention paid to the natural environment. After all, one purpose of green power is safeguarding nature.

Lower Energy Costs One of the benefits of hydroelectric plants is their cost. Instead of buying costly coal or natural gas, hydropower relies on the dependable, abundant natural resource of water. Hydropower plants are much cheaper to run than coal-fired plants with similar capacities for power generation. The world's largest hydroelectric dam is China's Three Gorges Dam. In what ways do you think building a large dam might hurt a region and its residents?

5 WAVE POWER

Wind and tides churn the surface of Earth's oceans, creating powerful waves. Have you ever experienced the power of an ocean wave? Those waves, like the water used in hydroelectric dams, contain large amounts of energy. Several promising technologies may turn wave motion into an important source of renewable power.

WAYS TO USE WAVE POWER

Try Wave Propulsion One of the potential uses of wave energy lies in **propulsion**. In 2008, a 69-year-old Japanese man named Ken-ichi Horie traveled 4,350 miles (7,000 kilometers) on a boat propelled entirely by harvested wave energy. Fins on the boat produced power by moving up and down with the motion of the waves. The eco-friendly *Suntory Mermaid II* powered

its lights and navigation systems with solar panels. The venture highlighted wave energy's bright future.

"Renewable energy is the source of energy for the future....This can create an industrial revolution and a lot of opportunities for jobs and research."
–*Manuel Pinho,*
Portuguese politician

Develop Wave Energy Plants The world's first commercial plant using wave energy to generate electricity opened in 2008. A Scottish company called Pelamis Power installed three 750-**kilowatt** machines that look like sea snakes just off the Atlantic coastline of northern Portugal. When ocean waves pass by these giant tubelike devices, they bend. Small motors inside the tubes convert the energy of the bending tube into electrical power for thousands of nearby homes onshore. Can you think of any disadvantages to this source of power?

Pump and Clean Water In addition to generating electric power, wave energy can accomplish physical tasks, such as pumping water from place to place. For example, wave-energy pumps can transport water into **reservoirs** for later use. Some wave-energy plants also remove the salt from seawater, making it safe to drink.

6 TIDAL POWER

As the Moon circles Earth, its gravity tugs at the oceans. This causes tides to rise and fall. Tidal power creates movement in coastal waters around the world. In some places, the tides are very strong. This energy, called tidal power, can be converted into electricity. As long as the Moon is in the sky, there will be tidal power.

WAYS TO USE TIDAL POWER

Develop More Tidal Turbines

Humans have recognized the enormous power of tides for thousands of years. Today, there are several ways to capture the energy of tides. One method is building a kind of dam, or barrage, that spans a coastal inlet. These barrages can convert tidal power into electricity, but they can damage the fragile marine environment. A cheaper, low-impact, and more successful approach to using tidal power is installing turbines underwater.

Support Tidal Energy Projects

In 2007, Verdant Power began work on the first major tidal energy project in the United States. The company anchored submerged turbines in New York City's East River. When the river's strong current broke several turbine blades, workers replaced them with improved versions. The company plans to install 30 turbines that would provide up to 1 **megawatt** of electricity for New York City. Check an electricity bill to see how many kilowatts of electricity your family uses a month.

Improve Tidal Technology

Tidal turbine technology is fairly new. More power is potentially available from the wind and the Sun than from tides. However, researchers, businesses, and government leaders around the world are working to develop and fund this promising green energy.

"We can build a low-carbon economy while unleashing American entrepreneurs to save the planet, putting optimism back into the environmental story."

–Michael Bloomberg, mayor of New York City

7 NUCLEAR POWER

Nuclear power uses **radioactive** metals to produce electricity. Reactions involving these metals produce heat. The heat is used to create steam, which turns electricity-generating turbines. Nuclear reactors also produce potentially dangerous radioactive waste. For this reason, it is the most troublesome renewable energy source. The nuclear power industry has improved safety in recent years, but challenges remain.

WAYS TO USE NUCLEAR POWER

Release No Greenhouse Gas Emissions

Even small amounts of nuclear reactor fuel contain vast amounts of energy. In 2008, the United States produced more nuclear-generated electricity than any other nation on the planet. This

energy accounts for 20 percent of the country's total electricity use. Nuclear power is completely carbon-free. Using nuclear power to generate electricity produces no greenhouse gases.

Dispose of Radioactive Waste Safely

Some of the waste from nuclear reactors remains radioactive for tens of thousands of years. Scientists have found no completely safe method to dispose of this waste. Still, many governments and industries rely on nuclear power. What do you think about this energy source? Do the benefits outweigh the risks?

Mine with Less Damage

Nuclear reactors require fuel, usually uranium. This fuel must be mined and refined before use. The large-scale mining of uranium often disrupts local ecosystems. Another concern is the amount of fossil fuel required to operate heavy mining equipment. Efforts are needed to reduce the environmental impact of mining.

"As Congress considers policies to address air quality and the...effects of carbon emissions on the global ecosystem, it is reasonable—and realistic—for nuclear power to remain on the table for consideration."
–Barack Obama, as a U.S. senator in 2005

8 GEOTHERMAL ENERGY

Earth's core is hot and **molten**. In places where Earth's crust is thin, this heat comes close to the surface, sometimes even breaking through as hot springs, geysers, or volcanoes. Earth's heat, called **geothermal energy**, can be used to power electricity-generating turbines. It can also be used directly to warm buildings or to heat water.

WAYS TO USE GEOTHERMAL POWER

Find the Geothermal Energy

Like nuclear and solar thermal power plants, geothermal power plants rely on heat to produce steam. The power of the steam under pressure turns turbines that generate electricity. However, for geothermal power, the source of heat is Earth itself. Geothermal activity is often present along the edges of large sections of Earth's surface, called tectonic plates. These plates are always moving. Iceland, located right over the edges of two plates called the mid-Atlantic ridge, gets a huge portion of its energy from geothermal power. The country's volcanic activity in 2010 is proof of its geothermal strength. What examples of geothermal energy have you seen in the natural world?

"[Geothermal energy has] huge potential...both as a solution to climate change and in terms of national energy security."
–Martin Ferguson, Australian minister of resources and energy

Support Geothermal Projects

Today, geothermal power accounts for only 0.3 percent of electricity globally. The world's largest geothermal power-generating project, the Geysers in northern California, gets its energy from natural hot springs. The Geysers' 15 power plants produce power for several nearby counties.

Use Ground Source Heat Pumps

People can use the direct heat of geothermal energy. A new innovation called a ground source heat pump is becoming popular in cold regions. The pumps draw tiny amounts of heat from the rocks below a building to heat the inside air. These pumps require small amounts of electricity to run. Residents almost anywhere can take advantage of ground source heat.

9 WIND POWER

The Sun's rays heat Earth unevenly. Air moving from hotter areas to cooler areas produces wind. Harnessing moving air provides another endless source of energy. It is called wind power.

WAYS TO USE WIND POWER

Develop Wind Turbines

Wind turbines operate much like tidal turbines. As air moves past a turbine, it pushes the blades, turning a shaft in the turbine and generating electricity. Most wind turbines are set atop tall poles. There, it is usually windier than at ground level. In 2009, wind power accounted for only two percent of the world's electricity. Government funding helps nations such as Denmark, Spain, and Portugal produce more than 10 percent of their power through wind generation. If you had money to fund a new green technology, which would you choose?

"As yet, the wind is an untamed, and unharnessed force; and quite possibly one of the greatest discoveries hereafter to be made, will be the taming, and harnessing of it."

–*Abraham Lincoln, 16th U.S. president*

Use Wind Pumps

A wind pump is a pump moved by a windmill. Many farms around the world use wind pumps to bring groundwater to the surface for irrigation or to provide water for farm animals.

Experiment with Turbines

Small turbines can be placed on roofs of buildings or on balloons high above the ground. Turbines can even float. In 2009, a Norwegian company installed the world's first full-scale floating wind turbine in the North Sea. "[We want] to test how wind and waves affect the structure, learn how the operating concept can be optimized, and identify technology gaps," explained a company official.

10 NEW FRONTIERS

As with any field, there are many ways to be creative with green energy. New technologies and types of power generation are being developed every day. The potential for great advances in the field of green power is enormous.

WAYS TO POWER THE FUTURE

Support Biofuels Green technology companies continue to explore **biofuel** possibilities. Biofuels are renewable fuels, such as biodiesel and bioethanol, that come from organic material. Those materials include corn, sugarcane, vegetable oil, or animal fat. Even pond scum might be a source of renewable fuel. In 2010, the U.S. government pledged financial support for research and development of algae-based fuels.

Investigate Uses in Space Groups of solar cells are called solar arrays. Spacecraft and space stations use solar arrays as power sources. Today, the International Space

Station's eight pairs of 115-foot (35-meter) wings are covered with solar cells. They power this orbiting laboratory.

"Electric power is everywhere present in unlimited quantities and can drive the world's machinery without the need of coal, oil, gas, or any other of the common fuels."
–*Nikola Tesla, inventor and scientist*

Invest in New Ideas

Texas businessman T. Boone Pickens hopes to produce the world's largest wind-power farm. He believes people are too dependent on fossil fuels. The project has faced setbacks, including a lack of transmission lines to deliver electricity generated from the wind farms to customers. What interesting new ideas do you have for green power?

10 Of the World's Largest Renewable Energy Projects

Green City
Abu Dhabi, United Arab Emirates
The Masdar Initiative is a private and public project to build a planned city in Abu Dhabi. Some $15 billion have been set aside to create a zero-emission, zero-waste city for 50,000 people and 1,500 businesses.

Offshore Wind Farm
Outer Thames Estuary, Great Britain
At a cost of more than $4 billion, ocean-based wind turbines are expected to power as many as 750,000 homes. When the project is completed, it will consist of more than 340 turbines.

3 Wind-Powered Building
Manama, Bahrain
The Bahrain World Trade Center, built in 2008, is the first skyscraper of its kind. Ocean winds, channeled between two towers, turn turbines that generate 10 percent of the complex's total power needs.

Tidal Power Turbine
Strangford Lough, Ireland
The turbine in Strangford Lough generates 1.2 megawatts of power. It is the largest tidal turbine in the world.

5 Tidal Power Barrage
Bretagne, France
Completed in 1967, the Rance tidal barrage is the largest tidal power plant in the world. It cost about $134 million to build.

ARCTIC OCEAN

NORTH AMERICA

PACIFIC OCEAN

8

ATLANTIC OCEAN

SOUTH AMERICA

N
W E
S

Scale: 621 Miles
0   1,000 Kilometers

SOUTHERN OCEAN

Countries around the world are researching, developing, and funding the building of renewable energy projects of all kinds. Here are some of the world's largest renewable energy projects.

Geothermal Power
North Sumatra, Indonesia
At a cost of $600 million, the Suralla Project will take advantage of Indonesia's active volcanoes to generate between 330 and 360 megawatts of power.

Solar Thermal Plant
Kramer Junction, California
The world's largest solar power facility is located in the Mojave Desert. It produces up to 350 megawatts of electricity.

Photovoltaic Power Plant
Olmedilla de Alarcón, Spain
This plant uses 162,000 solar panels to produce 60 megawatts of electricity. It is the largest photovoltaic power plant in the world.

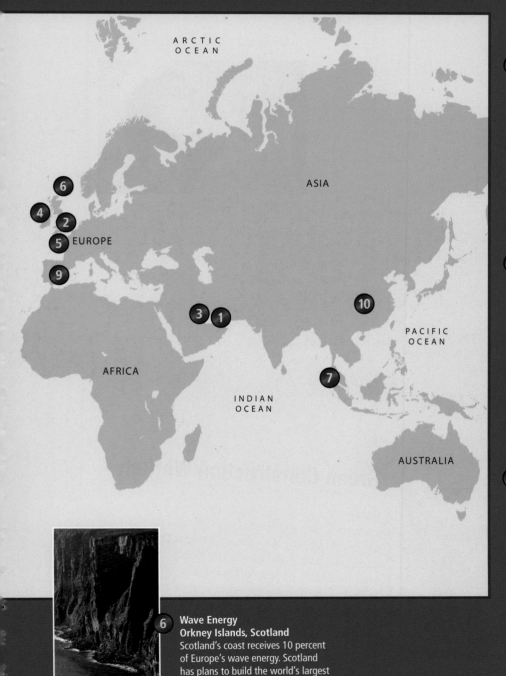

Three Gorges Dam
Chang (Yangtze) River, China
Built at a cost of more than $35 billion, the world's largest hydroelectric dam generates as much hydroelectricity as 15 coal-burning power plants.

Wave Energy
Orkney Islands, Scotland
Scotland's coast receives 10 percent of Europe's wave energy. Scotland has plans to build the world's largest wave energy harvester.

Green Careers

The key to sustainable energy use is planning. Workers with the skills to help make the switch to green power will be in great demand.

Green Engineer

Career

A green engineer collects and analyzes data, designs systems, and improves products and processes. At the same time, green engineers work to reduce the production of pollution and minimize risk to human health and the environment. Engineers close the gap between people and their needs. By designing products to fill specific needs, under specific conditions, green engineers are at the forefront of most of the green power fields. While some engineers work in offices and others work in the field, most do both.

Education

Becoming an engineer requires a bachelor's degree and often a graduate degree. Throughout their careers, engineers need to keep up with current technologies.

Green Construction Worker

Career

Every new energy-efficient, eco-friendly project needs hardworking people to put it all together. Whether assembling wind turbines in the North Sea or fitting solar panels in the Mojave Desert, construction workers do their part to make green buildings a reality.

Education

Construction workers need basic trade skills. In many cases, projects integrating the latest technology require specialized training.

What have you learned about Green Power?

Are you a green power expert?
Take this quiz to test your knowledge.

1 What is the difference between photovoltaic solar and solar thermal energy?

2 What are some drawbacks of nuclear power?

3 At what time in Earth's history were fossil fuels mainly produced?

4 Where was the first major tidal power project located in the United States?

5 Who sailed a wave-powered boat thousands of miles (kilometers)?

6 What are biofuels?

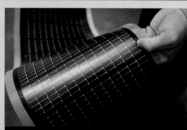

7 What is one advantage and one disadvantage of thin-film solar panels?

8 What is one of the best places in the world to collect geothermal energy?

ANSWERS: **1.** Photovoltaic converts sunlight to electricity, and solar thermal captures solar energy as heat. **2.** Harmful mining practices and radioactive waste **3.** The Carboniferous period **4.** East River, New York City **5.** Ken-ichi Horie **6.** Biofuels are renewable fuels, such as biodiesel and bioethanol, that come from organic material, including corn, sugarcane, vegetable oil, and animal fat. **7.** They are less expensive to produce, but they do not capture energy as well as PV cells. **8.** Iceland

Time to Debate

Should the world convert to using renewable energy sources?

Before changes are made that significantly affect people's lives and the economy, it is important to debate the issues involved. Making the switch from fossil fuels to green power, for instance, could cost many jobs and even put companies out of business. On the other hand, it will create new businesses and jobs in different areas.

PROS

1. Fossil fuels will dramatically increase in price and drop in supply in a matter of years.
2. After initial costs, renewable energy projects can provide power, profit, and employment for generations.
3. Using renewable sources rather than fossil fuels will reduce the environmental damage caused by humans.

CONS

1. The current systems of roads, sewers, and power grids use fossil fuels.
2. The initial cost of switching to renewable power sources is high.
3. Many new green technologies may prove to be unreliable.

WORDS TO KNOW

atmosphere: the layers of gases surrounding Earth

biofuel: a renewable fuel, such as biodiesel or bioethanol, that comes from organic material, including corn, sugarcane, vegetable oil, and animal fat

carbon dioxide: a heavy, colorless gas that forms when fossil fuels burn

carbon footprint: a measure of greenhouse gases produced by human activities

Carboniferous period: a geologic period that began about 360 million years ago during which forests covered much of the planet and enormous coal deposits formed

ecosystems: systems made up of living organisms, their physical environment, and the relationship between them

emissions: harmful substances discharged into the air, such as exhaust from cars

fossil fuels: fuels, such as coal, oil, or natural gas, that were formed hundreds of millions of years ago from plant and animal remains

geothermal energy: energy from the kind of power obtained by heat within Earth that is used to produce electricity or for other purposes

greenhouse gases: gases, such as carbon dioxide and methane, that trap heat when released into the atmosphere

hydroelectricity: electrical power generated from the force of falling or flowing water

kilowatt: a unit of power equal to 1,000 watts

megawatt: 1 million watts

molten: changed into liquid form by heat

propulsion: the force by which something is moved forward

radioactive: giving off harmful radiation

recycle: to process waste material so that it can be used again

renewable: referring to a source of energy that cannot be used up, such as solar or wind energy

reservoirs: natural or human-made lakes used for collecting and storing water

silicon: a nonmetallic chemical element found in sand and granite and used in metal mixtures, semiconductors, and building materials

sustainable: referring to behaviors and practices that preserve natural resources for use in the future

INDEX

Log on to www.av2books.com

AV² by Weigl brings you media enhanced books that support active learning. Go to **www.av2books.com**, and enter the special code inside the front cover of this book. You will gain access to enriched and enhanced content that supplements and complements this book. Content includes video, audio, web links, quizzes, a slide show, and activities.

Audio
Listen to sections of the book read aloud.

Video
Watch informative video clips.

Web Link
Find research sites and play interactive games.

Try This!
Complete activities and hands-on experiments.

WHAT'S ONLINE?

Try This! Complete activities and hands-on experiments.	**Web Link** Find research sites and play interactive games.	**Video** Watch informative video clips.	**EXTRA FEATURES**
Pages 12-13 Try this activity about hydropower.	**Pages 8-9** Link to more information about solar power.	**Pages 4-5** Watch a video about green ideas.	**Audio** Hear introductory audio at the top of every page.
Pages 16-17 Complete an activity about tidal power.	**Pages 10-11** Learn more about thermal energy.	**Pages 14-15** Learn more about wave power.	**Key Words** Study vocabulary, and play a matching word game.
Pages 26-27 Test your knowledge of the world's largest renewable energy projects.	**Pages 14-15** Find out more about wave power.	**Pages 20-21** View a video about geothermal energy.	**Slide Show** View images and captions, and try a writing activity.
Page 30 Complete the activity in the book, and then try creating your own debate.	**Pages 28-29** Learn more about green careers.		**AV² Quiz** Take this quiz to test your knowledge